UNCLE HANDSOME'S
REDNECK POETRY

THE
ROAD LESS
GRAVELED

BY BRENT HOLMES

ILLUSTRATED BY DON GILL

FATHER & SON

PUBLISHING, INC.

4909 North Monroe Street
Tallahassee, Florida 32303
http://www.fatherson.com
e-mail: lance@fatherson.com

and
The Redneck Poetry Company

ISBN: 0-942407-34-2

A portion of the proceeds from the sale of this book are contributed to the Minnie Pearl Cancer Foundation and Beyond Borders, a non-profit educational program which teaches literary and vocational skills to some of Haiti's most impoverished people.

Cover design by Bill Collier
Cover art by Don Gill

First Printing 1997, 10,000 copies
Second Printing 1998, 10,000 copies
Third Printing 1999, 10,000 copies
Fourth Printing 2003, 5,000 copies
Printed on acid-free, recycled paper

DEDICATION

To Heather Holmes, my pretty sister,
who has one of the best senses of humor I've ever known
(and who may never forgive me for dedicating
a book of "redneck" poetry to her)

And to Sarah Ophelia Cannon,
better known as Cousin Minnie Pearl,
for the many years of laughter she brought to our lives.

ACKNOWLEDGEMENTS

Bill and Gayle Collier, Rosalyn Holmes, David and Susan Holmes, David G. Holmes, Nancy Lewis, Don and Amy Martin, Bill and Martha Wolfe, Stuart Dill, Mark and Sally Hyatt, Connie Harrington, Jeanine Stevens, Judy Seale, Suzanne Hicks, Buddy Dukes, Ed Hicks, Dave Hoffner, Jamar Pillow and Zane Wine

Special thanks to the John Deere Co. for granting permission to use the John Deere trademark.
Special thanks to the Standard Candy Co. for granting permission to use the Goo Goo trademark.

TABLE OF CONTENTS

INTRODUCTION

Uncle Handsome likes to tell people that he lives near U.C.L.A. (that's Upper Central Lower Alabama). That is, in fact, where Uncle Handsome resides with his wife Eunice, his two boys, Big'un and Shooter, and Granny. They live on a gravel road a short ride south of the small town of Glory, Alabama.

As far back as I can remember Uncle Handsome has written poems and songs and an occasional story or two. Not long ago I shared some of his poems with some friends of mine. They loved them. Word got around and within a matter of months I was being asked to recite Uncle Handsome's poetry for various clubs and conventions. I was having a great time with it all when one day I heard a voice whisper, "Put the poems in a book....put the poems in a boook......."

I called Uncle Handsome. "Uncle Handsome," I said, "I think we need to make a book of your poems so more people can enjoy them. I'm driving through South Alabama on Friday. Do you have time to get together and talk about it?" "Why shore I do," he responded. "And if you'll meet me at that nice restaurant out by the highway at high noon I'll buy you lunch!"

I arrived early and was waiting in front of the restaurant when Uncle Handsome's tractor pulled into the parking lot. He was waving a handful of new poems in the air as he wheeled into a parking space.

As we visited over a nice long lunch I began reading Uncle Handsome's latest creations. Soon I was laughing so hard the people around us were beginning to stare. "These are great Uncle Handsome!" I exclaimed. "How do you do it?" "Well," he said slowly as he stirred his coffee with his knife, "I just watch Eunice, Granny and the boys and write things down as they happen mostly. Sometimes I'm moved to write when I'm watchin' a mule or tendin' the still or things like that. It just comes kinda natural really."

"Well, people sure do love them," I responded. "I've been having a great time traveling around and reciting them for folks." A look of deep contentment spread across Uncle Handsome's face. He leaned forward in his chair and said, "Well I'll keep writin' and you keep recitin'!"

We continued to visit and before I followed Uncle Handsome's tractor back to his place to visit with Eunice, Granny, Big'un and Shooter, we decided that putting together a book of his poetry was a good idea. That's how The Road Less Graveled began. We hope you enjoy it immensely.

Uncle Handsome's Favorite Nephew,

Brent

FOREWORD

HAAAAAAW!!!

Ardel, Bernel, Raynell, W.L., Lynell, Odell, Udell, Marcel, Claude, Newgene, Clovis and Jerry Clower all were raised close to a road less graveled. I read Uncle Handsome's redneck poetry to all my Ledbetter friends and they loved all of it. You could have no better review of this book than the Ledbetters.

When God turned that talent spout on Brent Holmes, he let it run awhile. This book of poetry proves it.

Jerry Clower

THE
ROAD LESS
GRAVELED

FATBACK

Fatback makes my griddle greasy
Makes my hen eggs go down easy
I'll eat it 'til I'm old and wheezy
Lord, I love good fatback

I love to sit and watch my wife
As she cuts it with her butcher knife
There ain't nothin' in this life
Better'n good ol' fatback

Grease poppin' high in the mornin' air
Gittin' on the walls and everywhere
There ain't nothin' can quite compare
With good ol' greasy fatback

I like it salty, never lean
Cut real thick and cooked with beans
I may not fit into my jeans
But lord, I love good fatback

Uncle Handsome

FROG GIGGIN' GRANNY

Granny says there's no thrill like giggin' a frog
Spottin' them suckers settin' on a log
Frozen in her headlamp's glow
She loves frog giggin', it thrills her so

When Spring rolls in and them froggies start croakin'
Granny sharpens her gigs while I set smokin'
Then she pulls out her waders and checks 'em fer leaks
Grabs some ol' croaker sacks and heads fer the creeks

Where she sloshes along thru the dark of the night
With her gigs held high 'til the froggy's in sight
Then straight as an arrow she lets her gigs fly
And the froggies they jump or the froggies they die

Granny likes her froglegs deep fat fried
With onions and 'maters settin' off to one side
Some folks kill chickens and some folks kill hogs
But Granny says there's no thrill like giggin' a frog

Uncle Handsome

A HOMEMADE
HONEYGLAZED HAM

I yelled, "Big'un! Git that pig off the porch
Before he comes in thru the door!"
But I was too late and he jumped thru the screen
And came trottin' 'cross the livin' room floor

I dove to catch him but he slipped from my grip
And I landed flat on my face
That pig went runnin' off into the kitchen
Snortin' like he owned the place

He went straight fer the flour sack 'n ripped it wide open
And the flour just flew everywhere
Then he found the syrup bucket and stuck his nose in it
And hoisted it high in the air

And the syrup in that bucket poured down on that pig
And splattered all over the floor
I hollered, "Quick, Big'un! Try to ease yer way around 'im
So we can git 'im back out the front door!"

That pig looked like he was in hog heaven
Wavin' that bucket in the air
Snortin' that satisfied snort pigs have
Slingin' sorghum syrup everwhere

Big'un got around him and we chased him outside
I said, "Now catch that rascal if you can!"
I said, "A syrup covered pig's just beggin' to become
A homemade honeyglazed ham!"

Uncle Handsome

DRIVIN' WITH NOTHIN' BUT THE RADIO ON

Eunice was nekkid as a jaybird
As she came runnin' up from the lake
Wavin' her arms like a woman gone wild
Yellin' somethin' 'bout a big water snake

She jumped up into the cab of the truck
And said, "Handsome, run git me my clothes!"
She said, "They're down there by that bucket of gizzards
With my snuff and my fishnet hose!"

And I pretended that I couldn't find 'em
As I wandered around near the shore
It must've made her mad 'cause the next time I looked
The truck wasn't there any more

I waited fer awhile but she didn't come back
So I started walkin' t'wards home
I laughed when I learned she'd been arrested fer drivin'
With nothin' but the radio on!

Uncle Handsome

ON BEIN' A POET

Bein' a poet's like trainin' a mule
It's somethin' that just takes time
I've written poems since I was a boy
Still too young to moonshine

Some folks think I'm different
But that's alright with me
A man's gotta do what a man's gotta do
He's gotta be what he's gotta be

So I let folks talk just as much as they want
'Bout me spendin' weeks with my rhymes
Heaven knows there's lots worse things
A feller could do with his time

'Cause a well writ poem's like a well trained mule
It's simply a joy to behold
It ain't worth as much but you don't have to feed it
Or worry 'bout it gittin' too old

And you don't have to worry 'bout it breakin' a leg
Or fallin' off into yer well
Or jumpin' yer fence or catchin' the colic
Or gittin' too pretty to sell

THE FRIDGES OF MADISON COUNTY

I found some ol' fridges in Madison County
And I set 'em up here by the swing
And pretty soon the porch there started to sag
But I never did do anything

And one afternoon when I was tryin' to tune
The banjo right there on the rail
I heard a loud crack and all of a sudden
That half of the porch just fell

My head hit a bathtub but I came to
Just as the dust settled down
'Cause Trailer started lickin' me right on my face
Then I thought about the rest of our hounds

But lucky fer them, they'd all been asleep
Under this side that's painted over here
And as soon as I realized that they were okay
A thunderclap cracked in my ear

And it started rainin' and the rain started runnin'
Off the roof and down onto my fridges
So I covered 'em up with a big orange tarp
I found down there where the bridge is

And now as I look at all of the damage
Those fridges have done to our home
I can't help but think I'd be much better off
If I'd left those ol' fridges alone

Uncle Handsome

12

ON BEIN' INSPIRED BY THE TREE ON THE ROOF

I was waterin' the tulips in the toilets out front
And was thinkin' 'bout life and truth
When I saw a little tree growin' up in the gutter
That's there on the edge of the roof

It was kinda tall with pretty green leaves
And was swayin' around in the wind
And it spoke to my heart 'bout bloomin' where yer planted
And survivin' and tryin' to fit in

'Bout branchin' out and holdin' on
Even when yer life's in the gutter
'Bout extendin' yer roots and holdin' yer turf
When the storm wind's a-shakin' the shutters

'Bout makin' the most of whatever yer given
And tryin' to reach fer the stars
All of these things came into my mind
As I was out there waterin' the flowers

I'm sure some folks wouldn't want a little tree
Growin' up on their roof like that
But it gives to me such deep inspiration
I'm leavin' that tree where it's at

Uncle Handsome

SHOOTER AND
THE MULE EGGS

Awhile back Shooter dreamed Ernestine layed an egg
Ernestine, our ol' swayback mule
The next mornin' he asked Big'un if mules layed eggs
He said, "Why Shooter, of course they do!"

Later that day while they were playin' on the porch
I took some coconuts and dipped 'em in wax
Then I made a big nest near the back of the barn
Where Ernestine always likes to relax

And I layed my mule eggs in the middle of that nest
Then I called little Shooter over to it
When he saw the eggs there he started jumpin' around
Shoutin', "I knew it! I knew it! I knew it!"

He said, "It's just like I saw in my dream last night!"
And now he's spent most of this spring
Sittin' on them mule eggs in the back of the barn
Tryin' to help Ernestine hatch the things!

Uncle Handsome

I TOOK HER FER GRANITE AND IT TURNED HER HEART TO STONE

Eunice is the nicest woman
I have ever known
But I took her fer granite
And it turned her heart to stone

Now I feel like a chunk of naughty pine
Like a dog without a bone
'Cause I took her fer granite
And it turned her heart to stone

Yes I took her fer granite
And now life sure is hard
'Cause I have to do all the cookin'
And mow this big ol' yard

Eunice won't do the washin'
Or mop these dirty floors
Or change my oil or slop the hogs
And now I'm doin' all the chores

Yes, I'm livin' in the doghouse
Eatin' my grits alone
'Cause I took her fer granite
And it turned her heart to stone

Uncle Handsome

GAME WARDEN KNOCKIN'
ON MY DOOR

Game Warden knockin' on my door
Game Warden knockin' on my door
Game Warden knockin' on my door
Should I let him in?

Has he come here to my house today
To cuff my hands and take me away?
Should I run or should I stay?
Does he want me or one of my kin?

I wonder just how much he knows
Did he see me shoot those does?
Or was it was it the turkeys?
You don't suppose the law could know
   about that?

My heart's a-poundin' in my chest
Should I hide those turkey breasts?
What if he finds all the rest
Behind that icebox door?

Game Warden knockin' on my door
Game Warden knockin' on my door
Game Warden knockin' on my door
Should I let him in?

Uncle Handsome

20

BELIEVIN' IN BIGFOOT

Believin' in Bigfoot's a strong tradition
In this little town I'm from
If you don't believe in Bigfoot 'round here
Folks kinda' figgur yer dumb

Now I've been a believer all my life
'Cause I saw him when I was a kid
'Course I didn't get a real good look at the thing
'Cause he ran so fast and hid

And the bushes were thick 'n my camera wouldn't click
And the tracks were messed up the next day
But I'm sure what I saw had to be a Bigfoot
I don't care what folks say

Yea, sometimes I feel sorry fer city kids
That never git out in the woods
And never git a chance to see a Bigfoot
Lord knows it would do 'em some good

'Cause it makes the world a mysteriouser place
And I don't know about ya'll
But I think we should start teachin' all little chillun
'Bout Bigfoots when they're small

Uncle Handsome

22

THEY COME FROM A FAR

They say the wise men come from a far
And I'm sure what they say is true
But I've often wondered about that far
And I 'spect you prob'ly have too

Did they build that far or were they puttin' it out?
Was it a house or a shed or a barn?
Or were they all campin' out and roastin' some weinees?
Or did they build it to keep themselves warm?

Follerin' stars and hangin' 'round fars
Someday folks are bound to realize
Spendin' time with friends in the great outdoors
Is a real good way to grow wise

Uncle Handsome

THE DRIVE THRU WINDER

I decided since I was already in town
I'd go thru a drive thru winder
And buy me a big ol' burger with cheese
Been so long I couldn't remember

So I ordered that burger and a couple of fries
And a big bellywasher to go
And I pulled on around to pick up my lunch
Real nice like and slow

And this big ol' boy handed out my food
Then he asked me about my ride
I said, "John Deere, 1947!"
And I pulled away with pride

Uncle Handsome

WHEN LIGHTNIN' STRUCK OUR OL' OUTHOUSE

When lightnin' struck our ol' outhouse
Granny was settin' inside
She came wobblin' out all sooty 'n smokin'
Lookin' like she'd just been fried

Her clothes had been burnt all over
There were holes in both of her shoes
We got her some water 'cause she looked kinda thirsty
We didn't know what else to do

Her hair was all singed and wirey
But soon she was talkin' quite sane
We stood there 'n stared at Granny in amazement
As the outhouse went way up in flames

I said, "We should rebuild it somewhere else"
But I could see Granny was agin it
She said, "Lightnin' never strikes the same place twice"
And since she was the one who was in it

We built it back right where it had been
But I guess Granny ain't too shore
'Cause I've noticed that ever' time it starts to thunder
She don't touch that outhouse door!

Uncle Handsome

28

THE NEW WINDERS

I heard folks talkin' 'bout a new kind of winders
So I drove to town to see fer myself
I asked a fella there, he pointed to a store
And said, "They've got the new version on the shelf"

So I went into the store and looked all around
It was full of computer stuff
But I didn't see any winders at all
And I'd pretty soon seen enough

But this fella walked up from behind the counter
He studied my boots and suspenders
Then he said, "Can I help you?" And I said, "Shore!
I'm tryin' to find the new winders!"

And he led me over to a computer that was there
And started pointin' out things on the screen
I couldn't understand a word he was sayin'
And I didn't want to treat him mean

But he kept talkin' that computer talk
And when I could finally stand it no more
I said, "If you don't sell winders fella, it's alright with me
'Cause what I really need to git is new doors!"

Uncle Handsome

BUFORD 'N MOMMA'S BRAZEER

I put a clothesline up between two of the bathtubs
Settin' out in the front yard
Momma was hangin' her underwear on it
When the wire started actin' real tar'd

And saggin' real low 'n Buford saw his chance
And went runnin' out 'n grabbed her brazeer
And went trottin' off with it hangin' from his mouth
Momma yellin', "Buford! Come back here!"

But Buford kept runnin' with his head held high
And Momma chased him down to the church
Just as a weddin' rehearsal was endin'
And some fellas in fancy white shirts

Tried to help Momma catch ol' Buford
And I'm sure they'll tell it fer years
How the bridegroom ripped a hole in his britches
Chasin' Buford 'n Momma's brazeer

And how the best man finally grabbed that brazeer
And how Buford wouldn't let it go
So they played tug-o-war out on the church lawn
They say it was an awesome show

And they say the bride's brother finally got Buford
To drop it by grabbin' his ear
And now folks all over this county seem to know
'Bout Buford 'n Momma's brazeer

Uncle Handsome

ON FINDIN' A NEW HOUNDDOG

'Bout a month ago I saw a hound
Out near the county line
There was not a soul around
And I was wishin' he was mine

He reminded me of a dog I had
Way back when I was young
So I stopped my truck and called him to me
And he licked me with his tongue

He was such a handsome hound
And it felt so good to hold him
I knew he'd make a real good friend

And I'm still glad I stole him

Uncle Handsome

34

ACCOMODATION

Eunice said, "Honey, it's gittin' late
The next time we decide to celebrate
Let's do it when we have more time"

As I set beside her and said, "Alright"
She kissed me softly while the candlelight
Fell upon our jug of shine

And danced across her skin and hair
And reflected off her lips so fair
She filled me with such desire

In those moments of quiet tenderness
Her gentle words and sweet caress
Set my heart on fire

We could hear in the distance the familiar sound
Of a young whippoorwill out singin' his round
And listnin' fer the song of his mate

Eunice whispered into my ear
"It's gittin' kinda cool in here"
So I reached out and shut the tailgate

                              Uncle Handsome

THE RESURRECTION OF A RABBIT

Our cat drug up a rabbit it had killed
It does that now and then
Eunice said, "Handsome! That's the neighbor's rabbit!
It must've gotten out of it's pen!"

And before I could say, "What 'er we gonna do?"
Eunice took that rabbit to the sink
And started shampooin' that stiff bunny's fur
She said, "They've gone out of town, I think"

She said, "If we can clean it up and git it back in it's pen
Before they get home we'll be fine"
Then she said, "Git my blow dryer so I can fluff him up"
I thought she'd done lost her mind

But we fluffed him up nice and put him back in his pen
So he'd look like he died in his sleep
And the neighbors came home and didn't say nothin'
But when we saw 'em at the end of the week

They said, "The strangest thing happened while we were gone"
Eunice and I tried not to grin
They said, "We buried our rabbit before we left town
When we got home he was back in his pen!"

Uncle Handsome

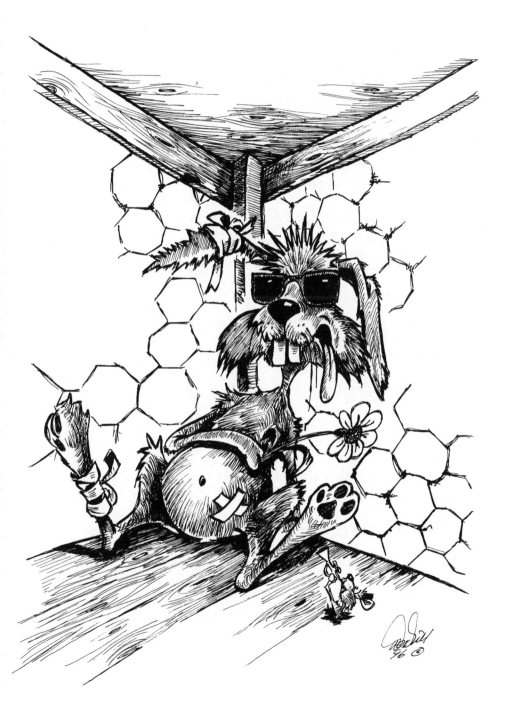

THE BACKYARD LANDFILL

We'd had our fill of goin' to the dump
And payin' to dump our trash
So we started usin' the ditch out back
And hangin' on to our cash

But then some buzzards started circlin' around
And Granny thought they might give us away
So she loaded her gun and shot one or two
But more of 'em came the next day

And she shot some of them but they came back again
And soon they were flyin' everywhere
I thought it was kind of inspirin'
The way them buzzards just filled up the air

It was more'n she could do to keep up with 'em all
And soon they were playin' cat and mouse
They'd circle real low 'til Granny walked outside
Then they'd soar real high o'er the house

And as soon as Granny'd come back in the door
They'd be down 'round our rooftop again
Them buzzards doin' that really got Granny's goat
And she'd run out and start shootin' again

Now Granny knew shootin' buzzards was against the law
But she told me she really didn't care
But when the Warden arrested her fer what she had done
She claimed that that wasn't fair

And they made Granny pay fer every buzzard they found
And it nearly brought her to tears
'Cause she knew fer what it cost to buy them dead buzzards
We could have gone to the dump fer years!

Uncle Handsome

THE MEANEST ROOSTER
IN THE WORLD

That's one mean rooster settin' over there
He'll run you right out of this yard
I've seen him chase off a pack of mad hounds
And he wasn't even tryin' hard

He sent the ol' bull runnin' out to the pasture
And he didn't come back fer ten weeks
I've watched him attack the neighbor's tractor
He claims that's why the engine leaks

I saw a chickenhawk try to kill that rooster
He hit him like a heart attack
Then he carried him off but he must've come to
'Cause he made that ol' hawk bring him back

Uncle Handsome

SANTA AND HIS LITTLE ELVIS

Little Shooter said, "Pa, does Elvis work fer Santa?"
I said, "No Shooter, who told you that?"
He said, "Big'un says Elvis makes toys fer Santa Clause"
It was more than I could do not to laugh

"Big'un said Elvis made the fishin' rod I got
And that Elvis made my new checkerboard
And that Elvis made the boomerang Santa brung to me
That broke out the winder next door"

"Big'un says Elvis is Santy's little helper"
I said "Shooter, Santa's little helpers are <u>elves</u>"
Shooter sat still and thought fer a minute
Then said, "How 'bout if we keep this 'tween ourselves?"

Uncle Handsome

EVER' TIME THE STILL GITS STRUCK BY LIGHTNIN'

Ever' time the still gits struck by lightnin'
It makes me kinda wonder
And think about the way things are
In the land that's over yonder

And I wonder if it's anything like
Life here on this planet
Heaven knows there's so much here
That we take too much fer granite

Like the wonderful smell of fatback fryin'
In the hours of the early morn
Or the satisfied look our ol' mule gits
When she's chewin' on an ear of corn

Or the purty colors of the tulips in the toilets
Settin' out in the front yard
If heaven is made of things such as these
Stayin' there won't be hard

Ever' time the still gits struck by lightnin'
It makes me cherish each day
And reminds me that I'm just passin' thru
Though I'd be right content to stay

Uncle Handsome

ON BUYIN' A CAR PHONE

I finally broke down and bought a car phone
'Cause the house gits so full of noise
With the TV set goin' and the dishwasher on
And Eunice and Granny and the boys

It's one of those things I wish I'd done
A long, long time ago
I never would've dreamed that a new car phone
Could change my little life so

I can sit out here and talk on this phone
Where everything's peaceful and still
And hear my friends like they're right beside me
Instead of way 'cross the holler or hill

Buyin' this car phone's 'bout the smartest thing
I reckon I've ever done
'Cause there's no place quieter than inside a car
Especially a car that don't run

                              Uncle Handsome

MOMMA'S WHOOPY CUSHION

I gave my wife a whoopy cushion
To honor our weddin' day
And the first time she set down on the thing
We laughed the night away

The next day Eunice used it on her boss
Thinkin' it would make him laugh
But she said he'd hardly finished cussin'
When he cut our income in half

Now I'm havin' to work twice as hard
And Eunice has time to kill
And all in all that whoopy cushion
Hasn't been such a big thrill

So if you're thinkin' 'bout buyin' one
Let me give you some friendly advice
Buy your wife some chickens or hole diggers
Or somethin' else real nice

Uncle Handsome

WHEN YER TRYIN' TO PICK BUCKSHOT OUT OF A BASS

When yer tryin' to pick buckshot out of a bass
You really have to concentrate
'Cause sure as you don't, later at supper
Someone'll jump from their plate

And yell, "Dang! I just bit into somethin' real hard!"
And whether they find it or not
You'll know good and well that what they just bit
Was a little bitty piece of buckshot

Why last night we had Cousin Quetester fer supper
And I was passin' the taters to my wife
When Quetester rared back a-holdin' her jaw
And started poundin' the table with her knife

'Course, bein' a lady she was tryin' not to cuss
The boys were tryin' harder not to grin
It embarassed Eunice right down to the bone
And she kicked me hard on the shin

'Cause she knew I'd cleaned that fish in a hurry
And I had no one to blame but myself
So if you can't take yer time when pickin' buckshot
Try to leave yer fishin' gun on the shelf

Uncle Handsome

A SPOTLIGHTER'S NIGHTMARE

I was videotapin' my favorite fishin' show
When I saw the Game Warden cross the lawn
I yelled, "Eunice! The Game Warden's comin' to the door!!
I'll hide in the kitchen 'til he's gone!!"

And as I waited in there I thought of all the critters
I'd killed while huntin' out of season
But why the Warden was comin' after dark
Was just a little more than I could reason

Then I heard the Warden knock and Eunice open the door
And invite him in real polite
Then I heard him say his truck had died down the road
And that he needed a good flashlight

Eunice pretended I was visitin' the neighbors
She said, "I know we don't keep one in here
Go look out there on the seat of Handsome's truck
And git that spotlight he keeps fer huntin' deer!"

Uncle Handsome

MULES, MAGNOLIAS 'N MOCKINGBIRDS

Mules, magnolias 'n mockingbirds
That's what the south is to me
I've heard tell of lots of other places
But there's no place that I'd rather be

'Cause there's nothin' like the smell of a magnolia flower
Or purtier'n a mule on a hill
Or sweeter'n the sound of a mockingbird singing
Perched on a limb near the still

Mules, magnolias 'n mockingbirds
Who could ask fer more?
As I write this poem I can see all three
Thru the crack in the outhouse door

                                    Uncle Handsome

BIG'UN AND THE BUCKTOOTHED BIGFOOT

Little Shooter came runnin' up all out of breath
He said, "Big'un saw a Bigfoot at the still!
He was ten feet tall and had buckteeth!
And went runnin' real fast 'round the hill!"

"He said he'd just started chewin' on a Goo Goo
When he saw him by the creek thru the trees!
Said it scared him so bad he couldn't even move
And he's still kinda weak in the knees!"

I said, "It's about time ol' Bigfoot came back"
But later I gave Big'un some grief
I said, "You shouldn't pull Shooter's leg like that
You know Bigfoot's don't have buckteeth!"

Uncle Handsome

GRANNY AND THE ULTRALITE CHICKENHAWK

Granny was huntin' groundhogs
With Aunt Edna in the field
When an ultralite buzzed by overhead

Granny thought the ultralite
Was a big chickenhawk
So she tried to shoot the thing dead

"Didja git it?" said Edna
"Didja git that ol' hawk?
Or was that just a great big ol' goose?"

Granny said, "It was a hawk
And I guess I just grazed him
But I made him turn that little fella loose!"

Uncle Handsome

CUDZU AT CHRISTMASTIME

We made a Christmas wreath out of cudzu vines
And we hung it on the outhouse door
And the kinfolk carried on about it so
That we made a whole bunch more

We put one on the shed and one on the barn
And three on the front porch screen
Then we strung cudzu around the satellite dish
Biggest wreath I'd ever seen

We put wreaths around our huntin' dog's necks
And we hung 'em o'er the doghouse doors
We even hung some on the sides of the fridges
Settin' out on the front porch

There was a time when I hated cudzu
I used to curse them cudzu vines
But now nothin' I know makes a place look better
Than cudzu at Christmastime

Uncle Handsome

62

U.F.O.'s

There's some Unidentified Frozen Objects
In the bottom of our old deep freeze
Like that beaver that I was too tired to skin
And that snake I found 'neath the trees

And froze 'til I could find someone
That knows somethin' 'bout stuffin' them thangs
Eunice won't reach down in there fer nothin'
She's afraid of them frozen fangs

There's a fox 'n a badger 'n a few other critters
That only heaven knows
My wife calls 'em, "Unthawed Mysteries"
But I call 'em, "U.F.O.'s"!

Uncle Handsome

64

THE BRIGHT ORANGE HUNTER

He came struttin' into the country store
Wearin' his bright orange vest
He had a bright orange hat 'n bright orange pants
And a bright orange shirt on his chest

He had bright orange gloves 'n a bright orange pen
That wrote with bright orange ink
We watched him as he bought his shotgun shells
We didn't know what to think

He had a bright orange belt 'n bright orange jacket
That sported a bright orange hood
He had bright orange boots with bright orange laces
I mean you could see him good

It was plain to us that this city feller
Had his head slap full of rocks
So I said, "Ain't you scared to walk thru the woods
A-wearin' them dark colored socks?"

Uncle Handsome

EATIN' GRANNY'S PEANUTS

When the Parson set down beside Granny's bed
She smiled her toothless smile
And even though Granny'd been right sick
They talked fer quite awhile

And as they talked I happened to notice
How the Parson was helpin' himself
To a big bowl of peanuts beside Granny's bed
A-sittin' there on the shelf

When Granny saw what the Parson was doin'
She said, "Finish 'em off if you wish"
She said, "I cain't eat 'em, I just suck off the chocolate
And put 'em back there in the dish!"

Uncle Handsome

TO PAT A HOUNDDOG
ON THE HEAD

When yer feelin' down and lonely
Like you should've stayed in bed
Sometimes it helps out a bit
To pat a hounddog on the head

When you git yourself tied up inside
'Cause of somethin' somebody said
It makes you feel a whole lot better
To pat a hounddog on the head

Hounddogs are good fer huntin'
And fer lookin' after yer yard
But they're also good fer makin' ya smile
When yer feelin' down and tar'd

So the next time you start feelin' blue
Remember what I just said
And step out there on yer ol' front porch
And pat a hounddog on the head

Uncle Handsome

WE BURIED AUNT EDNA
IN THE FLOODPLAIN

We stood there in the pourin' rain
Wishin' we hadn't buried Aunt Edna in the floodplain
But that was where she wanted to be
Out 'tween Uncle Lester and that ol' willow tree

I swear we done what we thought we oughter
But then the river rose up and put 'em both underwater
And that river kept rollin' and washin' dirt away
And Edna and Lester come up out of their graves

Them watertight caskets buried down deep
Exploded to the surface 'n then started to creep
Out t'wards the main channel where the river runs fast
And the departed departed 'mongst the carp 'n the bass

But then the dead rose again and continued to float
I yelled, "Big'un, run yonder and fetch us the boat!"
And we follered them caskets a-prayin' and a-hopin'
They didn't run into somethin', bust loose and come open

Aunt Edna couldn't swim even when she was alive
And if that casket'd come open there's no way she'd survived
The current was swift and the current was strong
But we chased them two caskets purt 'near the night long

We caught up with Edna up under a ridge
And lassoed Uncle Lester by a log 'neath a bridge
We tied up them caskets and we towed 'em to town
And we buried 'em both way up on dry ground

I know they's both Christians, they's washed in the blood
And if they ever rise again, it won't be from no flood

Uncle Handsome

POSSUM STEW

Set down friend and line yer flue
With a great big bowl of Momma's possum stew
It'll cure what ails ya and makes ya blue
It'll put a real fire in yer veins

It'll give ya the strength ya been needin' to plow
And to cut firewood 'n fence in the cow
And fix up the shed and butcher the sow
Ain't nothin' like possum stew

This stew's been known to make blind men see
It cured the coondogs when they wouldn't tree
No matter what pains ya it'll shore set ya free
Ain't nothin' like possum stew

It'll make ya so strong and make ya so brave
You could send a mad bear runnin' back to it's cave
It'll give ya the strength to git what you crave
Ain't nothin' like possum stew

One little taste and you'll know what I mean
You'll stand a foot taller 'n feel like a king
It may smell funny 'n look kinda green
But ain't nothin' like possum stew!

Uncle Handsome

THE FROG IN THE NOG

Shooter came runnin' up and said,
"Big'un took a frog
And dropped it over there
In that bowl of eggnog!"

He said, "I saw him!
He did it on purpose!"
I could see the frog's eyes
Pokin' up thru the surface

So I eased over close
To that bowl of eggnog
And when no one was lookin'
I grabbed fer that frog

But he dove under quick
Like I figgered he would
And my hand made a splash
As I missed him good

So I reached my hand deeper
Down into that drink
And was feelin' around
But then quick as a blink

That frog jumped out
All covered with cream
I'd never heard
So many women scream

As that nog covered frog
Made his way 'cross the floor
Half drunk and jumpin'
His way t'wards the door

I said, "Let 'im go Shooter,
Don't catch that ol' frog
We've done more than enough
Just by savin' the nog!"

Uncle Handsome

GRANNY AND THE HAUNTED OUTHOUSE

A woodpecker started peckin' on the outhouse door
While Granny was settin' out there
She kept yellin', "Wait just a minute!
Just a minute and I'll be out of h'yar!"

But that bird kept peckin' and Granny kept yellin'
The boys were just rollin' on the ground
When Granny came out she was mad enough to fight
But of course there wasn't no one around

She looked to the left and she looked to the right
Then she walked off actin' undaunted
Now she takes her shotgun when she goes out there
'Cause she figgers that outhouse is haunted!

Uncle Handsome

COLD, COLD BUTTERMILK

I sit and think about my past
As I stare into this big tall glass
Of cold, cold buttermilk

I think of all the roads I've follered
As that buttermilk waits there to be swallered
Cold, cold buttermilk

Cold 'n thick and kinda lumpy
Cheers me up when I feel grumpy
Cold, cold buttermilk

As my thoughts drift back in time
Many warm mem'ries flood my mind
Of cold, cold buttermilk

Settin' on the porch or here by the far
There's nothin' like a big ol' cannin' jar
Full of cold, cold buttermilk

Uncle Handsome

CARS ON BLOCKS

Cars on blocks, cars on blocks
Ain't nothin' like cars on blocks
Settin' over here, settin' over there
Cars on blocks settin' everwhere

Settin' out there in the mornin' sun
Still settin' there when the day is done
It's been years since any of 'em run
Ain't nothin' like cars on blocks

So full of rust and dust and dents
They stand in our yard like monuments
'Tween the pink flamingos and the white tire fence
Ain't nothin' like cars on blocks

Up on them blocks without any wheels
They give the ol' place a homely feel
Cars on blocks are harder to steal
Ain't nothin' like cars on blocks

Uncle Handsome

LIFE IN THE COUNTRY

Granny was chasin' a chicken snake
With a chunk of firewood
Shooter was runnin' from a big bumblebee
That had just stung Buford good

Big'un was scratchin' some fire ant bites
He got while walkin' to school
Eunice was swattin' at a huge horse fly
As she saddled up the mule

I was watchin' all the goin's on
As I lay 'cross the front porch swing
Thinkin' to myself, "Life in the country
Shore is a wonderful thing!"

Uncle Handsome

ON LEAVIN' THE CHRISTMAS LIGHTS UP

We leave our Christmas lights up all year long
'Cause they brighten up the neighborhood
And remindin' folks of Christmas Day
Is just bound to do 'em some good

A bunch of our neighbors used to complain
They'd say, "Do you always have to leave 'em blinkin'?"
Guess they finally realized all the good we were doin'
And changed their old ways of thinkin'

This year we left a sleigh on the roof
But the wind took three of the deer
And now some red birds have made a nice big nest
Up there in that ol' Santa's beard

We can sit in the yard and watch the momma bird
As she lands on that bald Santa's head
Then hops down into that beard full of babies
A-hollerin' out to be fed

By the time Christmas comes those baby red birds
Will have flown from that ol' Santa's beard
But our Christmas lights are gonna still be blinkin'
'Cause we leave 'em up all year!

Uncle Handsome

WHAT IS TIME TO A HOG?

A fancy feed salesman
Came knockin' on my door
He said, "Can I see yer hogs?"
And I said, "Shore!
Ain't got but three"
He said, "That's OK"
He said, "How old are they?
And what do they weigh?"

"They're six months old
And about thirty pounds"
He nodded his head
And kinda stared at the ground
And we walked to the hog pen
And after we stopped
He said, "Whateya feed 'em?"
And I said, "Slop!"

He said, "On my feed they'd weigh
Three hun'erd by now
And in a couple more months
They'd be bigger'n a cow!"
I knew right then
He had a head full of fog
So I asked that feller,
"What is time to a hog?"

Uncle Handsome

A LITTLE PROSE 'BOUT
FROZEN CLOTHES

As I look thru the winder at the sleet 'n the snow
And listen to the wind as it blows and blows
I stare out there at the frozen clothes
Hangin' out there on the line

Eunice hung 'em there when the weather was nice
Now they're solid as rocks 'n covered with ice
I started to git 'em once or twice
But they're still out there on the line

There's longhandle underwear 'n Momma's brazeers
And thirteen ol' socks that I've worn fer years
And a good Sunday shirt I ordered from Sears
Hangin' out there on the line

Gittin' 'em now would be kinda hard
That's why they're still out there in the front yard
Stiffer'n boards and heavier'n lard
Hangin' out there on the line

I shudder when I see those cold metal snaps
Out there on the back of them longhandle flaps
They're probably colder'n the polar icecaps
Hangin' out there on the line

Uncle Handsome

FISHIN' WITH THE WARDEN

The Warden kept seein' me pull up to the dock
With the biggest bass in the lake
And after awhile I guess it got to him
It was just a little more'n he could take

He said, "Handsome, you mind if I ride with you tomorrow
So you can show me how you fish?"
I smiled at the Warden and said, "That'd be fine!
Bring a friend or two if you wish!"

And he showed up early and we motored on out
To where we were way out of sight
And I shut off the motor and pulled out my lighter
And lit a stick of dynamite

Then I threw it overboard and it exploded in the water
And the fish started floatin' to the top
I grinned at the Warden as he stuttered and stammered
I thought he was gonna go into shock

Then he yelled, "Handsome! Yore under arrest!"
I said, "Arrest me if you wish"
Then I lit a stick of dynamite and tossed it to him
And said, "You gonna talk or you gonna fish?"

Uncle Handsome

SHOOTIN' PINK FLAMINGOS

This mornin' ol' Granny decided she was tar'd
Of them pink flamingos in the neighbor's yard
She said, "Look here, I'm gonna have me some fun"
And she reached 'neath the sofa 'n pulled out her gun

And went struttin' 'cross the yard in her boxers 'n her socks
To where that Camaro's been settin' up on blocks
And she clumb up there on it and she set on the hood
Then she thumbcocked that shotgun and aimed it real good

And blew one flamingo way up in the air
When I close my eyes I can still see it there
Kinda slow motion like, spinnin' over 'n over
Slowly fallin' to the ground, and lyin' dead in the clover

Granny looked at me with her gold toothed grin
Then she eyed another bird 'n aimed her gun again
Blam! And that pink flamingo went flyin'
And arched 'cross the hedges where the laundry was dryin'

And landed on Brummy 'n he run like the dickens
Straight under the porch a-scatterin' the chickens
'Bout then the neighbor started yellin' out her winder
And Granny shook her gun and threatened to send her

The way of her flamingos so she quit her yellin'
And went 'n run her hogs in on Granny's watermelons

Uncle Handsome

THE WASP ON THE WALL

Eunice had just settled down in the tub
When she noticed the wasp on the wall
She said fer a second it just set there
But then it commenced to crawl

And all of a sudden it took to the air
And started flyin' all over the room
Eunice was yellin' like her pants were on fire
Sayin', "Handsome! Run bring me the broom!"

She was more nervous than a longtailed cat
In a room full of rockin' chairs
As she sank to her chin in that tub full of suds
While that wasp flew around in the air

She kept yellin', "Hurry up Handsome!
Hurry up and kill this thing!"
I yelled, "Eunice, I think Big'un left the broom
At the neighbor's house last spring!"

And I opened the door just as that wasp
Was divin' down t'wards the tub
Eunice was yellin' as she went underwater
Tryin' to hide herself 'neath the suds

She waited down there just as long as she could
Then she came up a-gaspin' fer air
I said, "Eunice, that ain't no dadburn wasp!
That's a dirt dauber flyin' 'round there!"

Uncle Handsome

ELVIS IS IN OUR OUTHOUSE

Big'un likes playin' the banjo in the outhouse
He thinks that he's Elvis out there
Granny plays her flattop on the front porch
Where she can git lots of fresh air

Sometimes I fiddle in front of the fire
While Shooter plays a tune on the jug
Eunice will git a rhythm goin' on the bones
Rockin' in her chair on the rug

Sometimes we all git together and sing
And it shore does make me feel proud
But we never git to sing together too long
'Cause the hounds start bayin' too loud!

Uncle Handsome

FLAMINGOS IN THE MANGER SCENE

There's flamingos in our manger scene
We put 'em there this year
Leavin' 'em standin' off by themselves
Just seemed a little queer
With them other critters all gathered 'round
A-worshippin' the baby Jesus
Them flamingos stayin' across the lawn
Just somehow didn't please us
So we pulled 'em up and set 'em there
'Tween the wise men and the manger
Some folks think it's a little strange
But I've seen a whole lot stranger
I reckon they do stand out a bit
Bein' so pink and all
But the way they sway on one leg in the hay
They look so handsome and tall
Folks from town'll come drivin' around
And they'll slow way down and grin
At them flamingos there with the camels 'n donkeys
And them three fancied up wise men
And every now and then folks'll stop their cars
And come stand by our white tire fence
And take pictures and laugh at our pink flamingos
But to us it just makes sense
For all of God's critters to gather together
And worship at this time of year
And now that I stop to think about it
We left out the plastic deer!

Uncle Handsome

100

THE ROAD LESS GRAVELED

Two ol' roads split off in the woods
And I took the road less graveled
And my truck got stuck out there in the muck
And my wife kinda came unraveled

But then she got to lookin' at some wildflowers
Growin' by the side of the road
And she mellered out and apologized to me
Fer actin' like such a toad

And I managed to git the truck goin' again
And we drove thru the hills and the hollers
I wouldn't take the mem'ries we made
Fer a bushel full of greenback dollars

We got lost twice on that rutty ol' road
But we didn't really much care
We even stopped fer awhile to take a little nap
And got awakened by a big black bear

That bear started stickin' his nose thru the winder
Thinkin' we might have some food
Eunice came slidin' way across the seat
It put her in a real foul mood

So we headed home just as fast as we could
But of all of the roads that we've traveled
There hasn't been one where we made more mem'ries
Than we did on the road less graveled

Uncle Handsome

About The Author

Brent Holmes is a singer, a songwriter and a humorist. He lives near Nashville, Tennessee on a pleasant piece of land which he shares with one horse, one cat and two sheep. His humorous songs have been recorded by Ray Stevens, Jerry Clower, Minnie Pearl and Williams & Ree. This is his first book.

About The Artist

Don Gill is known at his local coffee shop as one of the great cowboy cartoonists in Gooding County, Idaho. Don is also a cattleman, a sorry team roper and an ex-buffalo hunter. He calls Gooding, Idaho home. Don and his wife Denise raise bramers, kids and who knows how many dogs. Although Don has been a cowboy all his life, after illustrating this book of "Redneck" poetry, he's decided the only difference between cowboys and rednecks is the hat.

A portion of the proceeds from the sale of this book are contributed to the Minnie Pearl Cancer Foundation and Beyond Borders, a non-profit educational program which teaches literary and vocational skills to some of Haiti's most impoverished people.

What folks are saying about
The Road Less Graveled

My neck has been red from driving a tractor, working on our farm, and from working a shovel, doing everything from laying sewer pipe to building. So, I take the term redneck as a term of praise, though I recognize most city-slickers don't intend it that way. The slick preacher that Granny got the drop on and the game warden that Uncle Handsome out-slicked and out-fished are people I know, as are Granny and Uncle Handsome.

And after all, why in the world have we for 2,000 years left pink flamingoes out of the manger scene? I was raised to believe that all of us are sinners and all of us need Jesus. And I don't know that any creature escaped "The Fall". So, I'm glad that Uncle Handsome is doing for pink flamingoes what somebody should have done for them in the last twenty centuries.

I studied at Scotland's oldest university and taught at one of America's finer universities, but the highest of my education has not come in higher education. It's come from the country folks at home who have instructed me. It is from these people that I have learned the most. And if Brent Holmes will let you stop laughing long enough to think, you'll find lessons worth learning in this book too.

Roy Herron
Tennessee State Senator

What folks are saying about
The Road Less Graveled

Behind, underneath and deeply woven into these lines of straight forward humor, we hear the memory ghosts of our grandmothers and grandfathers laughing their way through the world.

Ed Hicks
English Department Chair
Troy State University

What folks are saying about
The Road Less Graveled

Uncle Handsome is the type of man that is every game warden's nightmare. He probably never had a fishing license or hunting license in his life, but has always lived off the land (both his and everyone else's!).

> Walter Tatum,
> Chief Biologist,
> Alabama Department of
> Conservation and Natural Resources

What folks are saying about
The Road Less Graveled

This book is two things; it's informative, it's enlightening and it's hilarious!

Traylor Parker

Ernestine says, "save the following pages for emergency use."

Save this page for emergency use.

Save this page for emergency use.

Save this page for emergency use.

Ya'll come back now, ya' hear?

Put a little poetry in your ears!

You can listen to the author recite all 51 poems
in this book by ordering the audio version on
cassette or CD today.

To order additional copies, make ckecks payable to:
Father & Son Publishing, Inc.
4909 North Monroe Street
Tallahassee, Florida 32303

Please process my order for the following books, C.D.s and cassettes:

The Road Less Graveled Book _____ copies @ $ 9.95 _____
The Road Less Graveled C.D. _____ copies @ $ 14.95_____
The Road Less Graveled cassette___ copies @ $ 11.95_____
Bear Tunes for Kids C.D. _____copies @ $ 14.95 _____
Bear Tunes for Kids cassette _____ copies @ $ 11.95 _____
Beary Christmoose C.D. _____copies @ $ 14.95 _____
Beary Christmoose cassette _____ copies @ $ 11.95_____
Cow Tunes for Kids C.D. _____ copies @ $ 14.95_____
Cow Tunes for Kids cassette _____ copies @ $ 11.95 _____
Fun Tunes for Kids C.D. _____ copies @ $ 14.95 _____
Fun Tunes for Kids cassette _____copies @ $ 11.95_____
Fun Tunes for Teachers C.D._____ copies @ $ 14.95 _____
Fun Tunes for Teachers cassette ___ copies @ $ 11.95_____
MooseBeary Jam C.D. _____copies @ $ 14.95_____
MooseBeary Jam cassette_____ copies @ $ 11.95_____
Moose Tunes for Kids C.D. _____ copies @ $ 14.95 _____
MooseTunes for Kids cassette _____ copies @ $ 11.95_____
Sea Tunes for Kids C.D. _____ copies @ $ 14.95 _____
Sea Tunes for Kids cassette_____ copies @ $ 11.95 _____

Shipping and handling:
$3.00 for first product + $2.00/additional product $ _____
Florida residents add 7% sales tax $ _____
Enclosed is my check in the amount of $ _____

Name _____

Address _____

City_____ State _____Zip_____

Mastercard / Visa Card # _____

Exp. date_____ Signature _____

Phone _____
Or, if you prefer, Mastercard and Visa orders may phone 800-741-2712.

Fun Tunes for Kids®

"The Children's Music That Adults Adore"

To Order call: 1-800-356-9315
or use the coupon on the back of this page

www.funtunesforkids.com